GOD

IS

LIKE . . .

Children's Book About Ministry and God

Donald Mims

authorHOUSE®

AuthorHouse™
1663 Liberty Drive
Bloomington, IN 47403
www.authorhouse.com
Phone: 1 (800) 839-8640

Published by AuthorHouse 07/13/2020

ISBN: 978-1-7283-6662-3 (sc)
ISBN: 978-1-7283-6629-6 (e)

Print information available on the last page.

Any people depicted in stock imagery provided by Getty Images are models, and such images are being used for illustrative purposes only. Certain stock imagery © Getty Images.

This book is printed on acid-free paper.

Because of the dynamic nature of the Internet, any web addresses or links contained in this book may have changed since publication and may no longer be valid. The views expressed in this work are solely those of the author and do not necessarily reflect the views of the publisher, and the publisher hereby disclaims any responsibility for them.

KJV
Scripture taken from The Holy Bible, King James Version.

GOD IS LIKE...

A king on heaven's throne. In bible times, a king sat on a throne to give orders and to make decisions for the people. So to say, God is like a king on heaven's throne, means that he will command what will happen.

GOD IS LIKE...

A shield. A shield protected a soldier from the spear or arrow of his enemies. To call God a shield means that God will protect the people who trust Him.

GOD IS LIKE...

A warrior. He protects us and comes to our rescue when we are in trouble. When we feel afraid, scared, helpless, and when others threaten to hurt us, it's good to know God will rise up and come to our rescue.

GOD IS LIKE...

A shepherd. A shepherd loves and cares for his sheep. He watches over them closely and protects them from harm or danger. He also ensures that they have plenty to eat and drink. To say God is a shepherd means that he watches over us and protects us.

GOD IS LIKE...

A fortress. A fortress was like a walled city or fort where people went to be safe from an enemy army. To say that God is a fortress or a place of safety, means that he will keep us safe in times of harm or danger.

GOD IS LIKE...

A strong tower. Strong towers were built inside walled cities. If the walls were broken down, the people of the city would be safe inside the tower. A tower protected the people.

GOD IS LIKE....

A refuge. Some cities and forts were built on high, rocky mountain cliffs. It was hard for an enemy to attack a city like this. To call God a refuge means that we are safest when we have faith and trust him.

GOD IS....

Mighty and faithful. He created the entire universe and everything in it, such as the moon, the sun, the stars and everything on earth including us. God is everywhere at the same time. He has all power in his hands and he is all knowing.

GOD IS LIKE...

A caring father. This means God loves us very much just like a father loves his children. So to say that God is like a father means that he will protect us and care for us just like a father cares for his children.

GOD IS LIKE...

A lawmaker or legislator. He gives us rules to learn by such as the 10 Commandments to help us make good choices. God is good and he shows us in the bible how to do good.

GOD IS LIKE...

A caring mother. That means God loves us very much just like a mother loves her children. He will nurture and care for us when we are not well like a caring mother.

GOD IS LIKE...

A great friend. He will spend time with us and talk to us when we are lonely and sad. To say God is like a good friend means that he will spend time with us and be there for us doing good and bad times.

**THE
END**

GOD IS

God is omnipresent. To say that God is omnipotent means that God has all power to do whatever he wants to do.

God is omniscient. To say that God is omniscient means that there is nothing he doesn't know. He knows everything there is to know in our world.

God is omnipotent. To say God is omnipotent means that God has all power to do whatever He wants to do. There is nothing or no one stronger than God.

THE END

GOD IS GOOD
FOR OUR....

Physical Health: God makes us strong and resilient. Key Scripture: 1 Corinthians 6:19-20

Emotional Health: God's word makes or can help us feel better when we are sad. His word is good for the soul. Key scripture: 1 Peter 5:7

Spiritual Health: God's word can give us confidence and strengthen our faith in Him. Key scripture: Jeremiah 33:6

Social Health: God's word can lead us to the right people and friends. God's word can help us to enjoy life and have fun. Key scriptures: 1 Corinthians 15:33 & Proverbs 13:20

Printed in the United States
By Bookmasters